My Litt

of

N. L. P.

Neuro Linguistic Programming

Georges Philips
&
Tony Jennings

ISBN:
978-0953666775

Contact www.georgesphilips.com

Introduction

The proposition is quite straightforward. You have maybe a half-hour to spare and you want to know about NLP. That's about 6000 words to explain what makes people the way that they are and what makes them tick, i.e. to explain the how and the why of

People's identities

The beliefs people hold

The skills that they have or are able to acquire

The things that they do and do not do

The circumstances people find themselves in.

Just one little difficulty with this - it is not possible to explain NLP in 6000 words. Indeed, it is not possible to gain a proper understanding of NLP from a book of any length. To understand NLP it is necessary to

fully experience it; you cannot experience it by reading a book.

If you really want to understand NLP, the answer is to do the training. Naturally enough, we would like you to attend one of our own courses. The reality is that we are one of a number of reputable companies that provide training in NLP. The important thing for you is to select the company that you feel most comfortable with.

However, today is not about training, it is about reading. We can give you some information on NLP, a few of the headlines. If this is all you want for the moment, then this is the book for you.

The Headlines

- What is NLP?
- History Lesson
- Presuppositions
- How We Experience Life
- Well Formed Outcomes
- Rapport
- Modelling
- States
- An Introduction to Language Patterns

WHAT IS NLP?

NLP is about how people work, the nuts and bolts of human behaviour, the ingredients that go into making a human being.

Let's start with the words

N is for Neuro

This is concerned with the mind and the body and how they work together. There has for a long time been some understanding of the linkage between the nervous system and the brain. Work done under the banner of NLP and other research now suggest that the links between the mind and the body are much stronger than was previously understood. It may be that although the brain is Grand Central Station, trains of thought spread throughout the body.

L is for linguistics

This is about the language we use and hear. We listen to other people's words, we speak to other people and we use language to make sense of our experience. We think about the past, the present, and the future, in words. We speak to ourselves almost all of the time. In a world steeped in words, the language that we use is vital to our well being.

P is for programming

Think of computer programming and you have got this one. It is about how we programme ourselves to repeat patterns of behaviour. Often this can be very useful. Isn't it handy to be able to drive routine journeys while thinking about something completely different? Unfortunately some of our repeating patterns of behaviour are not useful to us.

From the unconscious to the conscious

NLP tells us that we have neural pathways running throughout the mind and the body, we use language to explain our experiences and we all have our own programmes that we run. Nothing particularly special about that - that is unless you can understand how it all works. And it does all work we do it all day every day. Indeed, a large part of the process of learning NLP is no more than drawing down many of your skills from the unconscious, having a look at them and perhaps improving them.

Identifying these skills gives you conscious access to them in the future. For example, you may regard yourself as having good intuition, being able to tell when someone is being dishonest with you. A useful skill to have.

NLP teaches that this "intuition" stems from your ability to pick up many different signals that are giving you the information that the person is being dishonest. NLP brings this ability into conscious awareness.

Summary

Neuro

How the mind/body works

Language

The words we use and hear

Programming

How we program ourselves

Unconscious to conscious –

NLP draws our unconscious skills into conscious awareness.

HISTORY LESSON

The origins of NLP are to be found in the University of California in the early 1970's. The founding fathers were Richard Bandler (who was a student studying mathematics and computers) and John Grinder, a Professor in Linguistics. It began as a study of excellence, i.e. what made the best the best. In particular they studied three therapists (there were always lots to choose from in California) Fritz Perls (gestalt therapy), Virginia Satir (family therapy) and Milton Erickson (hypnotherapy), all of whom were regarded as leaders in their fields.

By studying these three therapists they were able to identify the specific language, behaviour and supporting beliefs which each used in their work. Once identified, these language patterns, behaviours and beliefs were then modelled (you might call it copied). Once replicated, they could be taught. As a result other therapists were able to significantly enhance their success with clients.

As Bandler and Grinder had no background

in psychology or psycho-analysis they had not been trained to delve into the reasons **why** people do the things they do. Using what became known as NLP, their focus of attention was **how** people do things. An understanding of the components of how someone does something provides the potential for change.

In the years since Bandler and Grinder did their first work together many people have become involved in NLP and amazing advances have been made.

Summary

NLP originated in California, with Richard Bandler and John Grinder leading the way.

NLP examines how people do things rather than why people do things.

PRESUPPOSITIONS

It helps us to function if we believe that certain things are true. When we make some decisions before we do something, i.e. we pre-suppose, it helps us to perform the action. An example would be a soldier going off to war. It would be useful, at least from the army's viewpoint, if soldiers going off to war decided (pre-supposed) that their country was worth fighting for. Similarly, it is useful for a salesman to believe in his product.

It is important to understand that nobody is suggesting that presuppositions have to be "true". They are simply beliefs that it can be useful to have under certain circumstances. In thinking about presuppositions the question that should be asked is not "Is this true?" but "Would it be useful to believe this?" Take the example of someone going for an interview for a job. Two possible presuppositions would be

- I am going to fail
- I am going to succeed

We do not know whether either of these presuppositions is true but it is obvious which would be the most useful to have when going for the interview.

NLP has its own presupposition. No one claims that they are actually true, merely that it would be useful to act ***as if*** they are true. The way to test a presupposition is to act as if it is true and notice what happens.

Here are some of the most commonly quoted NLP presuppositions together with a brief explanation of the underlying point.

- The Map is not the territory.

A map of a hill is only a map; it is not the hill itself. We experience the world through our five senses. Information is drawn in through the senses and is then re-presented inside us - we draw an internal map of what is going on outside. It can be useful to remember that this re-presentation is only a map, not reality itself.

- People respond to their map of reality, not to reality itself. NLP is the art of changing these maps, not reality.

We respond to our internal map, not the world as it really is outside. As this is an internal process, we can change or exercise some influence over it.

- Mind and body are one integrated system.

Although perhaps radical at the time, the idea that the mind and body work together as a single unit is now widely accepted, even though the mechanisms are still little understood.

- People already have all the resources they need - including those necessary to make any desired change.

We all have untapped resources inside, that are hidden to us. NLP provides methods of tapping into those resources.

- The meaning of a communication is the message that is received.

It does not matter what you say to someone, what counts is what they hear. Put simply, if you ask for four hot dogs and the street trader thinks you asked for five, you can be sure that you will get five hot dogs. Similarly, if you wish someone well, they will make a judgement about whether you are sincere. That is, the message received will be dependent on the level of sincerity they think you have - and this may be very different from what you intended to convey.

- There is no failure, only feedback.

When something does not work for you there are always lessons that can be learned. We may enjoy our successes, we learn from our failures. It can be easier to do this if you think about the absence of success as being feedback rather than failure.

- If you always do what you have always done, you will always get what you have always got.

It is quite common for people to repeat patterns of behaviour even though they know that this repeated action does not give them the result that they want. You can spend your whole life making the same mistakes and getting the same results.

- Choice is better than no choice.

It can be an unpleasant experience when you feel that you are being forced down a certain road because you believe you have no choice. NLP shows how to expand the choices available to you. Even if you then end up going down the same road, you are doing it consciously, you are making a choice.

- People are doing the best that they can, given the choices they believe are available to them.

The reason why people are doing the things that they are doing is because they cannot think of anything better.

They are not aware of any alternative ways of behaving that would be more effective.

- Modelling excellence leads to excellence.

If you want to be really good at something find someone who excels at it then copy what they do.

- To change someone else, change yourself first.

If you behave differently with someone else you will get a different reaction from them, i.e. by changing your behaviour you can influence theirs. Also, making changes of your own is a much more practical proposition than trying to change someone else.

Summary

A presupposition is something that we pre-suppose, that is something that we decide about before we think or act.

It is not necessary to believe that presuppositions are true. However, it may be useful to act as if they are.

HOW WE EXPERIENCE LIFE

An imagined experience can seem as real as an actual event and its effect on you can be equally powerful. Mark Twain once said something like "I have had some terrible experiences in my life, and some of them have actually happened". The point he was making was that we have the ability to imagine to such an extent that we can upset ourselves. Parents waiting for their children to come home in the evening can be particularly good at this.

On the positive side, we can be equally good at imagining good things. For some people watching a TV holiday programme or reading through a brochure can transport them to the most beautiful locations in the world - in their mind.

In thinking about the future what we do, in effect, is to create it in our minds. We may run a movie, hear a conversation or experience what it would feel like to be in an imagined future. We experience what we create in our minds. And this is not confined to future events. We do the same with events in our past. The difference, of course, is that the process of looking forward involves imagining something that has not happened. When we are looking back, we are thinking about an event that actually took place.

Think about it this way. At some time in your past something unpleasant happened to you. For example, you may have been chased by a barking dog and have felt very frightened. So much so, that whenever you think about the experience, some of the fear that you felt comes back to you. So what is causing the fear? Is it the event itself, that may have happened years ago, or is it remembering the event - running the movie - that is causing the fear? The NLP answer is that it is the movie that is causing you the trouble.

This conclusion has wide ranging implications and is also very good news. What it suggests is that everything that happens outside of the "now" moment - that is you reading these words right NOW - we experience as a movie that we run in our heads. This potentially gives us some control. All we need is to take control of the movie, become our own Director.

Let us go back for a moment to being

chased by a barking dog. At the time we experienced the event through our senses. We saw, we heard, we felt, we smelt and maybe we even tasted fear. Looking back we re-experience the event in the way we recall it in our minds.

The interesting thing that NLP has found is that our response to these memories is determined by the structure that we create. For example, if you rerun the

movie of the dog, yet this time push the dog further back and lower the sound of the barking it is likely that remembering the event is a less frightening experience. Nobody is suggesting that at the time the dog was further away. What happened at that time is not important. It is not the event that is causing you to feel fear years down the line; it is your memory of the event. So why not play around with the memory?

You will not be surprised to hear that NLP has lots of ways of editing or reshooting our internal movies.

Summary

The only reality is the "now" moment. Everything else is either imagined or remembered.

We can change the way we imagine or remember things, if we want to.

WELL FORMED OUTCOMES

A definition of a fulfilling life could be that you achieve what you set out to achieve. Yet many people are unclear about what they want. They do not think positively and clearly about what they want, let alone draw up a plan of how they are going to get it. They may plan a holiday, a new kitchen, a new wardrobe. They may work to or even draw up Business Plans at work. However, planning to get what they want out of life is too often haphazard or non-existent.

One of the reasons for this is that many people only think in order to solve problems. They spend most of their time on automatic pilot, doing the things that they do. Then, when a problem arises, they work on it until they find a solution or some way around it. It is likely that you can think back to the last time you solved one of life's little conundrums, whether this was how to go about finding a new job or how to find some where to park the car. Can you remember the last time you woke up and gave serious consideration to how to make life better for yourself? It does not happen much.

One of the golden nuggets of NLP is Well Formed Outcomes. They provide a structured way to think positively about what you want and how to go about getting it. Here is a brief rundown of the procedure.

Step one

Decide what it is you want and state it positively. Many people can very easily describe what they do not want and this is not very helpful to them. The mind cannot deliver negatives, only positives. Be positive about what you want.

Step two

How will you know that you have got what you want? You need to have an evidence procedure.

Step three

Start and maintain.

Ask yourself how, specifically, will I start the process of getting what I want, what do I do first?

Also, how, specifically, will I maintain progress towards my outcome?

Step four

Put your outcome into context answering questions such as

When do you want it?

With whom do you want it?

Where do you want it?

How long do you want it for?

Step five

Retain the positive by-products. This involves thinking about your current behaviour or situation, and identifying what positive benefit you get from it. You can be sure that there is something. For example, a smoker may find a cigarette is a good excuse to have a break. Breaks are good things and need to be preserved. This step is about identifying your own positive by-products and working out ways to preserve them.

Step six

Ecology checks

Cost: Is achieving your goal worth the money it will cost (or you will lose) by achieving it?

Time: Is achieving your goal worth the time you will need to put into it?

Other relationships: How will achieving your outcome effect other people? Is this okay?

Step seven

Set into a wider context. This involves thinking about your outcome more broadly. Useful questions to ask are

What else will happen when I get what I want?

Might there be any undesirable by-products?

What will I have to give up to achieve my outcome?

What will I have to take on to achieve my outcome?

Step eight

The internal check. This is the most important check of all. It is where you go inside to understand how you truly feel about your outcome. Your gut reaction. Take time to be still and quiet and decide whether your outcome feels like the right one. Be wary of any "yes but" answers.

Summary

1. **What do you want? (stated positively)**
2. **How will you know when you have got it?**
3. **How will you start and maintain moving towards getting what you want?**
4. **Put your outcome into context.**
5. **Retain the positive by-products.**
6. **Is it worth the time and cost?**
7. **Put it into a wider context.**
8. **Final internal check.**

RAPPORT

Most of us have had the experience of meeting someone for the first time and finding that we are comfortable and relaxed with them almost immediately. You are in rapport with them and the dialogue and business between you flows easily and effortlessly.

For most people this is a naturally occurring phenomenon that happens from time to time. People working in the field of NLP have identified what is actually happening when two people are in rapport. Here are two of the more important elements.

Body language and Tonality

You would tend to think that in any meeting between two or more people it would be the words that are exchanged that would be the most important element. Not so. When we receive information we are much more likely to pay attention to the tonality and language being used by the person addressing us.

For example, if someone said that they like

you, yet said it in a sarcastic voice you are more likely to believe the sarcastic tone rather than the words that you hear. NLP emphasises the importance of using the correct tonality when you speak.

Similarly, if someone says "Yes" to you while at the same time shaking their head as if they were saying no then it is likely that the message you receive would be the "No" (the body language message) rather than the "Yes" (the word being used). NLP takes a close look at body language and what you can do to achieve greater levels of rapport with people you come into contact with.

Language

Another aspect of rapport is the words people use. It is much easier to build a good relationship with someone else when you are “both speaking the same language", that is you are both "speaking in the same way.

NLP makes much of the fact that we experience the world through our senses (Representational systems in NLP jargon).

Visual	**seeing**
Auditory	**hearing**
Kinaesthetic	**touch and feel**
Olfactory	**smell**
Gustatory	**taste**

Although our senses are working most of the time, the ones that we rely on most are our visual, auditory and kinaesthetic systems. However, we each have an individual preference as to the extent that we use these senses, how we process information. You can identify a person's preferences from the language that they tend to use.

The words that are used in language that are sensory based are called predicates in NLP jargon. A predicate is a word that tells you something about something. The predicates in the following sentences are in bold.

The sky is **clear.**

The air is **crisp.**

The surface is **rough**.

Of the three main senses (visual, auditory, kinaesthetic) people will have one that they prefer over the others. By listening to the language that they use you can tell what this is. The value of this is that once you identify their lead system you know something about how they process information. It is then simple for you to talk to them "in their own language". This will ensure that

(a) they understand more clearly what you are saying
(b) they will feel more in rapport with you

Here are some examples of things that people may say together with a matching response.

Statement

I can **see** that I will be successful in the future.

Matching response

Yes I think that you have a **bright** future.

Statement

My partner and I seem to be in perfect **harmony** these days.

Matching response

It's good to **hear** that you are getting on so well.

Statement

I feel so much better now that I am no longer under **pressure**

Matching response

I am glad to know that things are going more **smoothly**.

When you are addressing groups you are not in a position to match each individual's leading representational system. However, what you can do is to ensure that your presentation (whether oral or in writing) uses predicates from all of the representational systems. In this way you can be sure to reach everybody that you address.

If you would like to discover something about your own representational systems the following exercise will give you an indication of where your preferences lie.

For each of the following statements place a number next to every phrase using the following scoring system.

You may choose to note your answers on a separate sheet

3 = The closest to describe you

2 = The next best description

1 = The least descriptive of you

1. I decided to read this book because

	I felt it would be of benefit
	It sounded like it would be of benefit
	It looked like it would be of benefit

2. During an argument I am most likely to be influenced by

	The other person's tone of voice
	Whether or not I can see the other persons argument
	Whether or not I feel in touch with what the other person is saying

3. I most easily communicate what is going on with me by

	the way I dress and look
	the feelings I share
	the tone of my voice

4. It is easier for me to

	find the ideal volume and tuning on a stereo system
	select the most comfortable furniture
	select rich attractive colour combinations

5. When I first enter a crowded room I begin by

	having a good look round
	tuning in to what is going on
	getting a feel for the atmosphere in the room

Now copy your answers in the section below

1		2		3		4		5	
	K		A		V		A		V
	A		V		K		K		A
	V		K		A		V		K

Now add the numbers associated with each letter

	V (Visual)	A (Auditory)	K (Kinaesthetic)
Q.1			
Q.2			
Q.3			
Q.4			
Q.5			
Total			

The comparison of the totals will give you an indication of your relative preference for the major representational systems, visual, auditory and kinaesthetic.

Summary

Being in rapport allows you to build stronger and better relationships.

Three aspects of rapport are

- **Body language**
- **Voice tonality**
- **The words we use**

MODELLING

Modelling takes you back to the beginnings of NLP. Bandler and Grinder began by modelling other people. The original proposition was that if you could identify what it was that made the best the best, you could then teach it to others. The early work undertaken by Bandler and Grinder was all about modelling excellence. They talked about looking for the difference that made the difference.

Like most of NLP there is nothing radically new about this idea. We are all naturals at the art of modelling. It is just that most of us do not know it. What NLP does is to bring the skill into conscious awareness so that it can be examined, understood and done as a deliberate act.

As is the way with NLP, a lot of different techniques and strategies have been developed to help us to consciously model other people with the intention of being able to replicate excellence. For the purposes of this book, we intend to confine ourselves to looking at the modelling that we already do, often unconsciously.

For most of us our first role models are our parents. It can be very interesting to see the many similarities that sometimes exist between two generations, particularly fathers and sons and mothers and daughters. You can often detect similarities in

How they walk

How they stand and sit

How they talk

Physical mannerisms or habits

Their views/prejudices

Sometimes the child grows up to be a clone of one of the parents. More usually they will take on some of the parents characteristics, although not all of them. So where do other characteristics come from? Often the answer is other role models. These could be

Siblings (particularly elder ones)

Other relatives

Peers

Other significant figures in the child's life

Characters from books, films and TV (both fictional and non-fictional)

Some people would argue that everything we do and say is the result of copying. Physical mannerisms, the way we speak, even our beliefs and values may be copied from somewhere. We are individual only in the sense that we each have our own unique blend of models that we have drawn upon and used to a greater or lesser degree.

We are like a patchwork quilt, with all the individual pieces of material taken from other garments. We are our own particular mixture of materials, all borrowed from somewhere.

Modelling brings many benefits. It is how children learn to walk and talk. We can also learn

Respect of others

Self respect

How to succeed

How to love

How to be happy

However, because much of our modelling is done at an unconscious level we can equally learn

How to worry

How to be depressed

How to procrastinate

How to criticise

How to complain

How to be self centred

How to be angry

How to be detached

How to be unfulfilled

How to be unhappy

If you are good at any of these things you can be sure that you have spent time with someone who is an expert at them. Do you know who this is?

NLP enables us to see and examine how it is that we live our lives. It brings it into conscious awareness. With awareness comes choice. When you know that you have choice, you know that you can take control of your life. Do I want to be like this or do I want to change something?

If you want to make a change you can use NLP techniques and strategies to model alternative ways of being.

Summary

We are all naturals at the art of modelling.

We often model our parents and other significant people in our life.

Some of our modelling serves us well, some does not.

NLP provides a structured approach to modelling.

STATES

It is self evident that the quality of our life is determined by the state that we are in. At any given moment each of us are in some sort of state. Indeed, we all have a repertoire of states, some we are in regularly, others less often. The range of our repertoire also varies from person to person. There are a number of ways of describing our state. We can talk in terms of:

Our body - how we feel physically;

Our emotions - our internal kinaesthetic reaction to what we are experiencing;

Our mental state - our level of alertness and awareness, the amount and speed of our mental activity; and for some

Our spiritual state - the level of awareness of the relationship between ourselves and something larger than ourselves.

Think about the states you are in at different times of your life

Lying on a beach

Stuck in a traffic jam

When you first wake in the morning

Doing exercise

Relaxing after a meal

Your Baseline State

Although we all have a range of states that we move between, we each of us also have a baseline state, i.e. a state in which we spend most of our time, a state where we feel most at home. You may never have considered this state before. Yet now that you are, you will be able to go inside and become aware of the characteristics of your own baseline state.

As you are so very familiar with your baseline state, it feels like home. Yet this does not mean that everyone's baseline state is comfortable. While someone's baseline state may be very tranquil, it could equally be agitated, on guard, or anxious. Similarly, your baseline state could involve a high degree of muscular tension, or your body may be in a more relaxed state. Some baseline states may not be very pleasant. However, they will all feel very familiar to the individual. If you would like to find out more about your own baseline state you may like to run through this exercise.

Begin with a few minutes quiet contemplation so that you can familiarise yourself with your baseline state. You will be able to get a good sense of it, what you look like, what you sound like (listen to the sound of your voice), and what you feel like. When you have this information move to the questionnaire.

Part One

A description of your baseline state	
How does your body feel physically?	
What are you feeling (emotionally) inside?	
How would you describe your mental state?	
How would you describe your spiritual state? (if applicable)	
What adjectives would you use to describe your baseline state to someone else?	

Part Two

Where does your baseline state come from? Did you learn it from someone else? If so, from whom?	
Did you learn it consciously or unconsciously?	
Is it the baseline state that you want?	
How would you describe your ideal baseline state?	

The Art of State Management

People who can manage their states are successful and in control of their lives. It is the difference that makes the difference. Think about how you view the world and the strength that you have to mould your own life on those days that you feel vibrant, happy and full of energy. Now compare this to how you feel about things when you are tired or feeling just a little unwell - how disempowered you can feel.

It is easy to see that if you could change states at will you would gain considerably more control over your life. You would be happier and more successful. Thinking about this in NLP terms the starting point would be, is it possible to change states? The answer, of course, is yes. We can do it in an instant. Most of us have had the experience of flying into a rage. At the other end of the scale, you may have had the experience of your heart melting in an instant - perhaps the sight of a new born baby.

As changing states is a naturally occurring phenomenon, that is something that we can all do, it is perfect for an NLP approach. NLP provides an insight into the process giving us the ability to change states, at will.

There are four steps.

Step 1 Understanding

An understanding of what components go into a state.

Step 2 Awareness

The ability to recognise and understand the state you are in at any given time.

Step 3 Alteration

The ability to deliberately alter your state, at will.

Step 4 Utilisation

This is about timing. Being in the right state at the right time and being able to use this more resourceful state to make a difference to your life.

Summary

We are always in some state or other. The one we are in most often is known as our baseline state.

By learning how to manage your states you can be happier and more successful.

The four steps to changing states are:

- Understanding
- Awareness
- Alteration
- Utilisation

INTRODUCTION TO LANGUAGE PATTERNS

NLP examines the language that people use every day to describe the world that they see, hear and experience. We turn the information we receive through our senses into words. Then we can think about things and discuss them with others or ourselves. However, there is a lot of information available to us. It has been estimated that there are about 2 million bits of information available to our senses at any given moment. Turning all of this information into language would be a massive task. So the mind goes through a process of condensing experience into language in three ways.

It deletes information

The mind is selective about the information it puts into words. We ignore much of the information available to us yet because the deletion takes place before we turn our experience into language we are not conscious of what we have deleted.

It generalises information

The mind uses its memory to compare information it receives with what has happened in the past and looks for recurring patterns. It then predicts what is going to happen in the future. This can be useful; it generalises that holding your hand too close to a flame hurts. It can be less useful if someone uses the generalisation "Everybody hates me".

It distorts information

We are the product of what we experience. Everything that happens to us helps us to form how we think about the world. Yet because everybody has different experiences we all think about the world in different ways. We all develop filters which we use to "make sense" of the world. These filters distort information. A classic example of distortion is to listen to two opposing sides of a conflict. Both will have honestly held yet completely different interpretations of events.

A particular form of distortion is the process by which people turn nouns into verbs. If someone says "I feel restless" they turn restless into something with a solid form. It is not. Being restless is an activity. To understand restless you need to turn it back into a verb. You might like to ask them to consider what is happening inside when they are feeling restless. Then they can think about restless as an activity, which is what it is.

We delete, generalise and distort the information available to us. So what? If we all do it, it's just the way things are.

While that is true, would it not be useful for us to be more aware of what we are doing in transforming what we are experiencing into what we are saying we are experiencing?

When we delete information it might be useful to know what we have deleted.

When we make generalisations it might be useful to challenge those generalisations.

When we distort information it might be useful to examine the way we have distorted the information.

NLP has developed ways to enable you to challenge deletions, generalisations and distortions.

Summary

We are use language with ourselves and to others to describe the world we live in.

In taking what we experience our mind

- Deletes Information
- Generalises Information
- Distorts Information

An understanding of language patters can help us to identify what has been deleted, generalised and distorted

Some closing words

So, there you have it, NLP in around 6000 words. If you read it all in one sitting you probably did it in around half an hour. If you missed them, it would be well worth your while spending another half an hour doing the two exercises we included.

Also, if you read the book in a single sitting your head is probably spinning. This is to be expected. We have given you a lot of information about how you and other people function - lots of food for thought. Let your mind chew on it for a while. It will all fit together for you eventually, and then you will see the sense of it.

You may also have a feeling of wanting to know more. We will hold up our hand and admit this was one of the intentions behind the book. We have a strong belief that a knowledge of NLP can allow you to get more out of your life, to be happier. We would dearly like for the world to be a happier place.

So, our closing words are a reiteration of what we said in our introduction. If you are at all interested in learning about NLP please get yourself in to a training course. It is one thing reading about NLP; it is quite a different proposition to see it, to hear it and to experience it.

Other books with

Georges Philips:

My Little Book of Verbal Antidotes
Georges Philips & Tony Jennings

Verbal Antidotes is a "must read" for anyone with the vaguest interest in self-improvement. Bestselling author Georges Philips has collaborated with Tony Jennings to produce a book that, to borrow a gardeners phrase, will shake the apples of your tree. Be assured, this book changes lives. Buy it for yourself. Buy it for your friends. It's that good.

My Little Book of Meditation
Georges Philips & Tony Jennings

For thousands of years man has been meditating. Now that we have a greater understanding of how the mind works the benefits of meditation are becoming more and more apparent.

More people than ever are learning to meditate and expanding their minds in the process. The benefits are not just limited to mental strength and wellness. They also include a reduction in stress levels and increase in physical well being.

Having read this little gem of a book you will have the necessary understanding to enable you to meditate with confidence.

The simple step by step instructions will demystify the art of meditation. You will enjoy the experience. Everybody does.

Change Directions
Perceive it, Believe it, Achieve it.

Georges Philips
Forward by Edward de Bono

The newest offering in the therapeutic and self-help field is, above all else, a very practical book on the process of changing direction. Its straightforward language and methodical, step-by-step approach makes the process easy to comprehend.

From analysing different situations involving change to going through the specific thinking and action steps needed in order to change direction, every detail and each step is clear and powerful.

His message is clear: it is your thinking fuelled by your determination that brings about a change of direction. Profound and actionable, this is the most compelling treatise on affecting personal growth and fulfilment to be published in recent memory.

Full of practical, easy to understand steps capable of transforming both your personal and professional lives, Change Directions: Perceive it, Believe it, Achieve it is as engaging as it is encouraging and enlightening.
Also available in Spanish.

About Georges Philips:

Georges Philips is a Neuro Linguist, Change Architect, psychoanalyst, author, trainer and performance coach. He has a private practice in London where he has worked since 1989. With his wife Lyndy, he teaches belief restructuring and Neuro Linguistics both in the UK and Europe. In addition Georges has written several books ranging from Analytical Hypnotherapy and Belief Restructuring to Neuro Linguistic Programming and Stress Management.

Georges is also a certified Edward de Bono trainer teaching thinking skills to organisations through the UK and Europe.

For training and coaching needs, contact via website.

www.georgesphilips.com

www.twitter.com/georgesphilips

www.facebook.com/gpabc

www.linkedin.com/georgesphilips

Printed in Great Britain
by Amazon